Blessed E

Four Anthems for

Margaret Rizza

RSCM

RSCM

The Royal School of Church Music
19 The Close, Salisbury, Wiltshire, SP1 2EB, UK
email: press@rscm.com Website: www.rscm.com
Registered charity 312828

Blessed Bread
Four Anthems for Communion
by Margaret Rizza

ISBN: 978-0-85402-197-0
RSCM Catalogue number: RA582
Order Code: A2336

Cover: The Last Supper (mosaic), Byzantine School, (6th century) / Sant'Apollinare Nuovo, Ravenna, Italy / The Bridgeman Art Library
Music origination by Donald Thomson
Printed in Great Britain by Caligraving Ltd

CONTENTS

1. Blessed Bread Page 4

2. The Real Presence Page 15

3. Dedication Page 20

4. Lord, all truth is from you. Page 25

PREFACE

This collection of four anthems for communion is made up of two very simple anthems with words by David Adam and two chants which can be used in many different ways according to the changeable time that is needed for communion and for the resources of the choir.

The Real Presence can be sung very simply indeed just as a unison song. But if wanted the indicated phrases could be sung by the men only and then by the women only. The scoring is for SATB, soprano descant and a melody instrument. Both the descant and melody instrument are optional.

Again the format for **Dedication** is the same. It can be used as a unison piece or as an SATB piece with optional descant and melody instrument.

Regarding the two chants I have numbered the actual chants which are normally 8 bars long to make it easier to skip according to the time one has available and also to take into account the resources of the choir. As a very simple basic example, in **Lord, all truth is from you**, one might start with the first 5 chants then skip the Double chant 6 if there are not many people going to communion or the group has no instruments, and pick up again on chant 7. You then might want to skip the Double chant 8 and pick up again on chant 9 going through to chant 10 to the end. In some communion services even if there are few people the whole chant can be sung as a time for prayer and recollection

The same applies to **Blessed Bread.** You may want to sing the first 4 chants but skip the double chant 5 if you have no instruments and then go to the Chorale chant 6. If you have no descant then you would skip the Chorale double chant 7 and go to chant 8. Then if you have no cello you would skip the double chant 9 and finish off with chant 10 into the end bars. With both chants you can repeat as much as you want especially if you need to extend the time and of course both can be sung as a unison version.

Chants are so easy to perform and also lovely to sing and to work at. Through the repetitions, a chant starts in the head with all its thinking and begins the long journey into the heart. There one begins to be open to the beauty of prayer, and drawn into deeper levels of reflection and stillness. Singing chants is a wonderful way to share, as we come to celebrate the Eucharist together.

Margaret Rizza
The Feast of St Aldhelm 2012

Blessed Bread

Margaret Rizza,
based on the Eucharist

Margaret Rizza

Chant 1

Flexible (♩ = c.76-84)

Chant 2

Chant 3

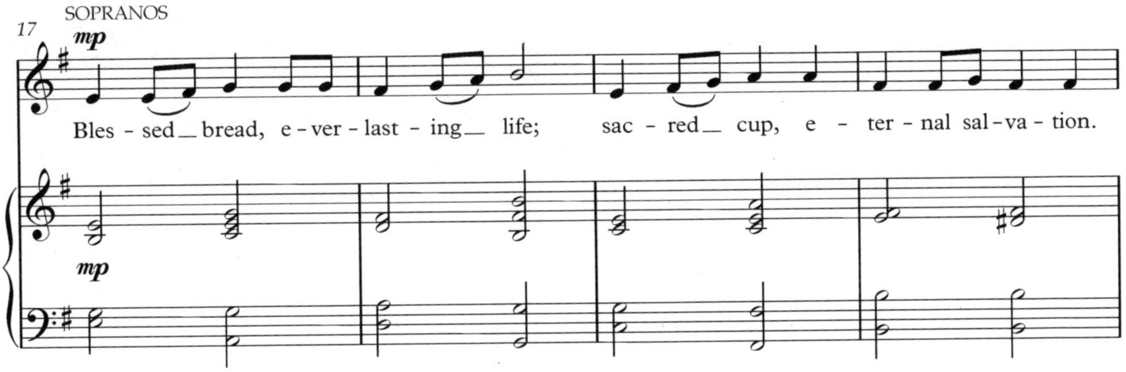

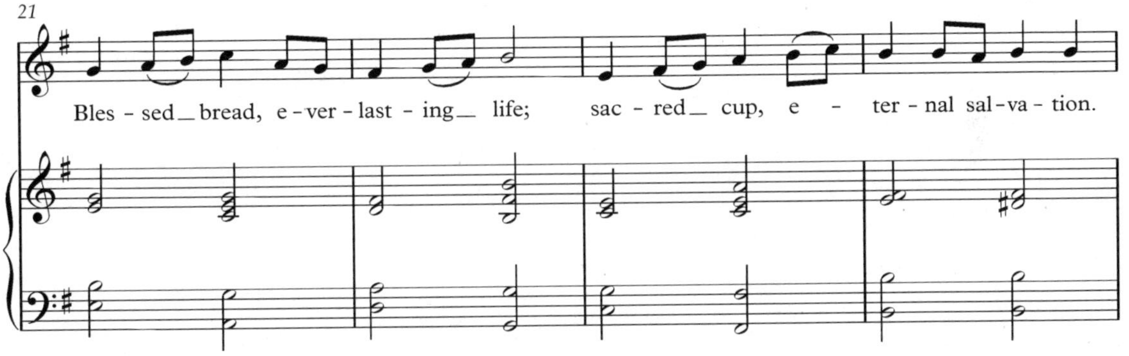

Chant 4

Double Chant 5

37
CELLO (Optional)
mp
41
Bles - sed bread, sac - red cup,
mf

Chant 6

Un poco meno mosso

CHORALE

Double Chant 7

61
ah,
bles - sed bread, sac - red cup.
65
ff
ah,
(ossia)
ff
Bles - sed bread, sac - red cup,
ff
ff

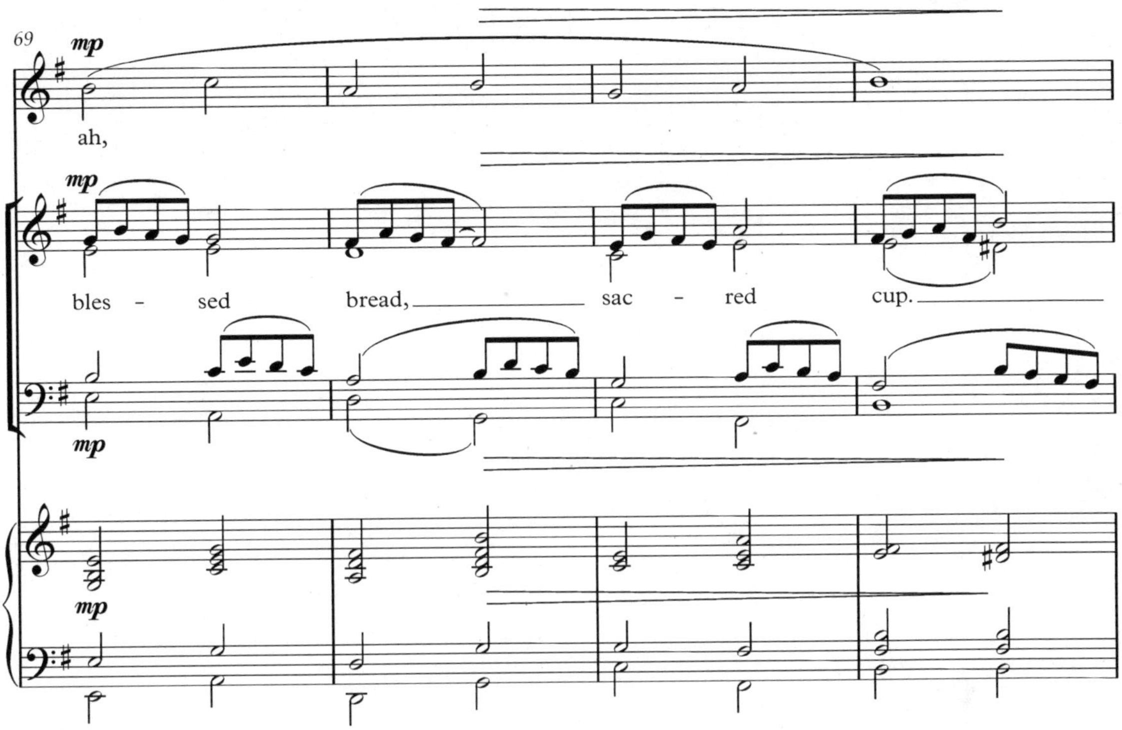

Chant 8

Tempo I

ALL VOICES IN UNISON

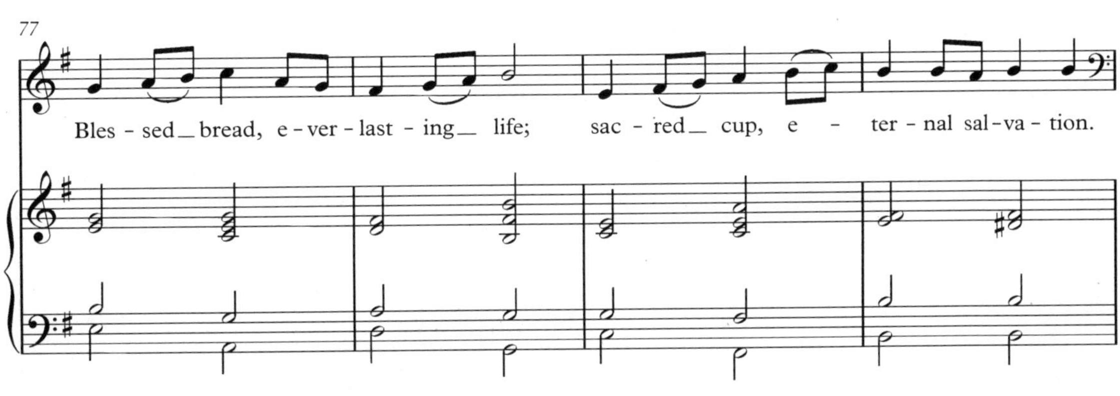

Double Chant 9

89
Bles - sed bread, sac - red cup,

93
bles - sed bread, sac - red cup.

Chant 10

97
S.
A.
p
Bles - sed bread, e - ver - last - ing life;
T.
B.
p
p
101
sac - red cup, e - ter - nal sal va - tion, e -
105
rit. al Fine
ter - nal, e - ter - nal sal - va - - tion.
rit. al Fine

The real presence

David Adam
from 'The Edge of Glory'

Margaret Rizza

This communion anthem may also be sung in an alternative unison version

(or UNISON)
13
mf
S
A
Lord, be___ with me in the break-ing of the bread. Lord, bless my heart, my
T
B
mf
mf
16
cresc.
hands, my head. Lord,_ be_with me, of-fer-ing the wine. Lord, bless bo-dy and
cresc.
(ossia)
cresc.
un poco rit.
a tempo
20
MELODY INSTRUMENT (Optional)
mp
dim.
soul, they are thine.
dim.
un poco rit.
a tempo
dim.
mp

TENORS and BASSES
25
mf
Lord, pre-sent in the wine and bread. Stay with me, Lord, when I am fed.
mf
SOPRANOS and ALTOS
29
mf
un poco rit.
Bless the way by which I go; guide me in this world be - low.
un poco rit.
a tempo
33
MELODY INSTRUMENT (Optional)
mp
a tempo
mp

DESCANT or MELODY INSTRUMENT (Optional)
Ah, ah,
S A
Lord, thou art there in bread and wine; a-round my life may
T B
(ossia)
ah,
thou en - twine. Bless O Lord, the life I lead, from

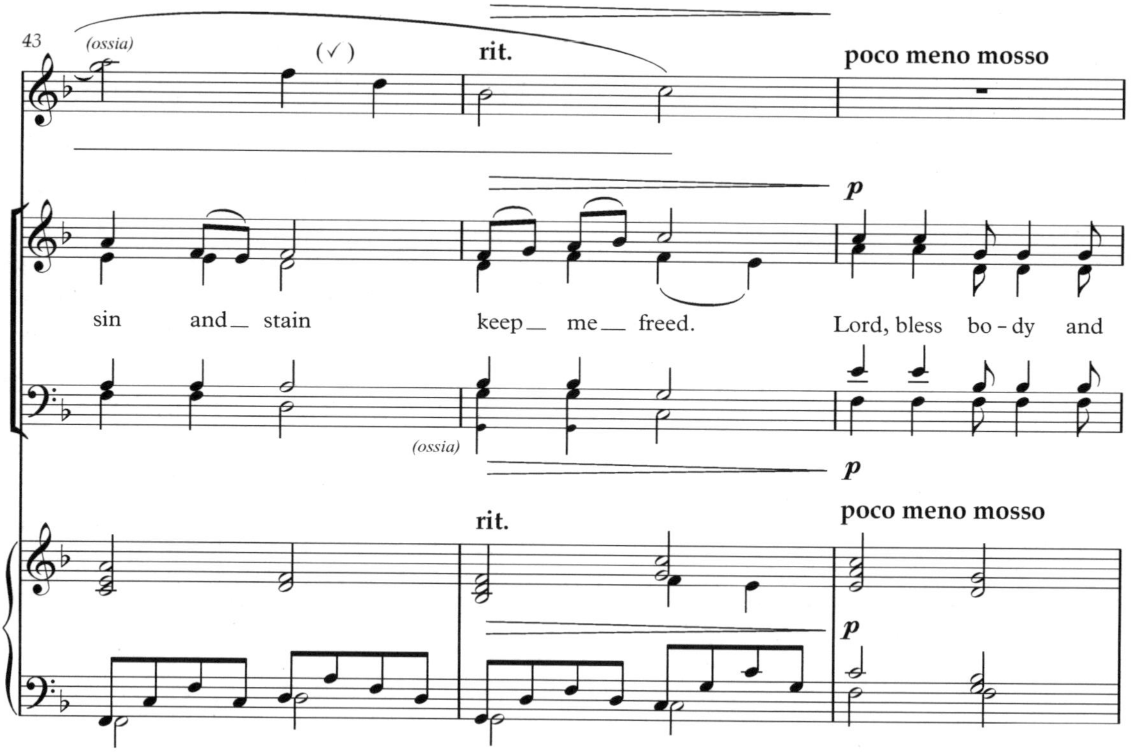
43
(ossia)
(✓)
rit.
poco meno mosso
p
sin and stain keep me freed. Lord, bless bo - dy and
(ossia)
p
rit.
poco meno mosso
p

46
molto rit.
soul, they are thine; Lord, bless bo - dy and soul, they are thine.
molto rit.

Dedication

David Adam
from 'The Edge of Glory'

Margaret Rizza

SOPRANOS and ALTOS
13
mf
(✓)
I give my-self to you, Lord, with my hands and their work - ing.
mf
17
mf
(✓)
S.
A.
I give my-self to you, Lord, with my mind and_ its__ think-ing.
T.
B.
mf
mf
21
(✓)
I give my-self to you, Lord, with my hands and their work - ing.

25 MELODY INSTRUMENT (Optional)
mf
3
mf
3
S: I give my-self to you, Lord, with my eyes and their see - ing.
29
mf
(✓)
S.
A.
p
'Ah' or Hum
T.
B.
p
Optional
'Ah' or Hum
33
p
(✓)
T: I give my-self to you, Lord, with my bo-dy and its act - ions.
mf
p
'Ah' or Hum

37
MELODY INSTRUMENT (Optional)
mf
3
mf

SOPRANO DESCANT or MELODY INSTRUMENT (Optional)
41
mf
(✓)
Ah,
f
I give my-self to you, Lord, with my heart and its lov-ing.
f
f

rall.
45
(ossia)
ah.
I give my-self to you, Lord, I give my-self to you, Lord.
rall.

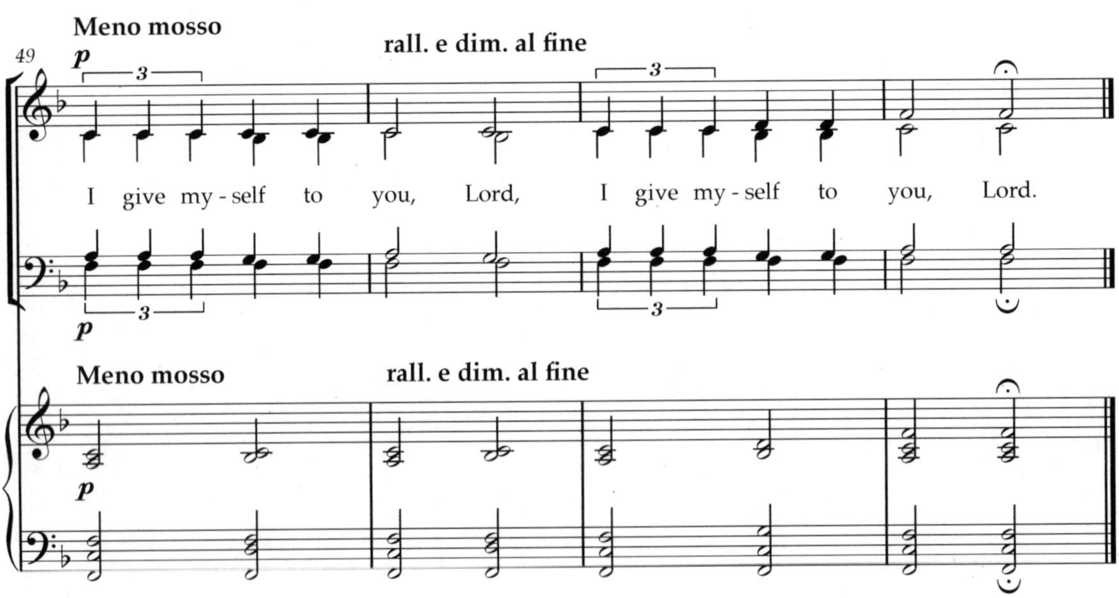
Meno mosso
49
rall. e dim. al fine
I give my - self to you, Lord, I give my - self to you, Lord.
Meno mosso
rall. e dim. al fine

Lord, all truth is from you

From the Weekday Missal Week XXI

Margaret Rizza

Chant 1

Largo, but flexible and flowing (♩ = c.50)

Chant 2

13
Give us a long-ing for your pre - sence and make us one with you.
Hum

Chant 3

17
mf
S.
A.
Lord, all truth is from you; on - ly you bring one-ness of heart.
T.
B.
mf
mf
21
Give us a long-ing for your pre - sence and make us one with you.

Chant 4

Chant 5

Double Chant 6

41 C INSTRUMENT DUET

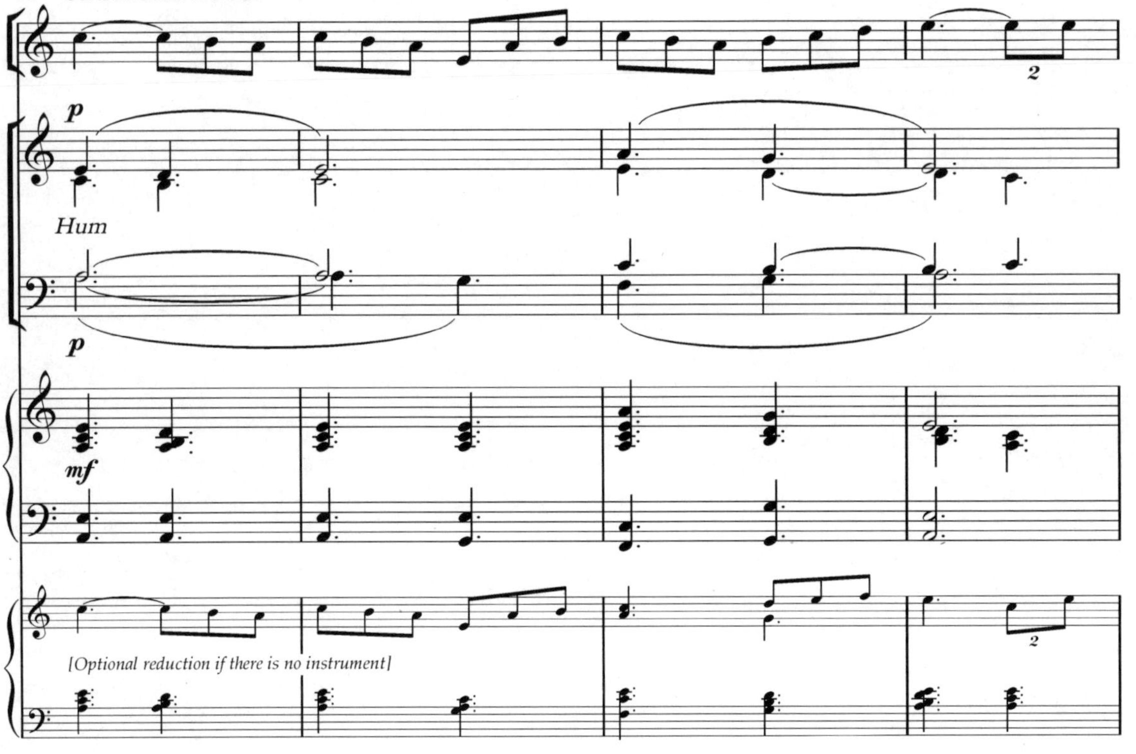

49
Hum
53
Hum

Chant 7

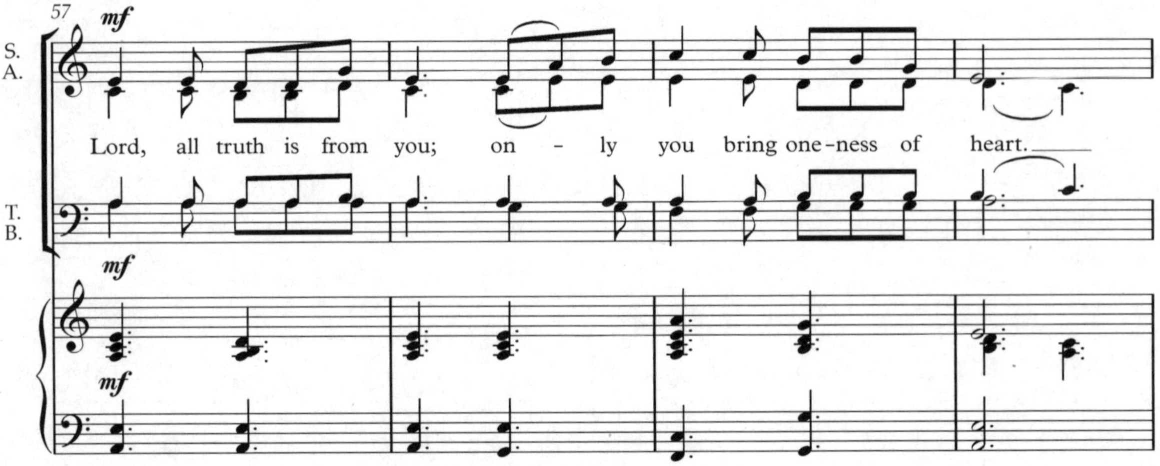

Double Chant 8

69
Lord of all truth, make us one with you.
Hum
73
Lord of all truth, you bring one - ness of heart;
p
Hum
p

77
2
2
2
2
2
Lord of all___ truth, make us one___ with___ you.
Hum

Chant 9

SOPRANOS SEMI-CHORUS
81
mp
Lord, all truth is from you; on - ly you bring one-ness of heart.
Hum
[Optional]

85
Give us a long-ing for your pre - sence and make us one with you.
Hum
Chant 10
89
Hum
molto rall. al fine
93
Hum

C INSTRUMENT VARIATION (duet)

FLUTES / RECORDERS

CELLO BASSO CONTINUO I

CELLO BASSO CONTINUO II (for full *f* rounds)

CELLO VARIATION I (with Organ Acccompaniment I)

CELLO VARIATION II (with Organ Acccompaniment I)